WRITTEN BY
PAUL MASON

ILLUSTRATED BY
SAM LEDOYEN

GREAT
SCIENTISTS

Contents

The hall of fame

Isaac Newton

My name's Isaac Newton. I am famous for my discoveries about light, gravity and the movements of the planets. It involved a lot of studying …

In 1661, Isaac arrived in Cambridge – ready to start university.

Trinity College that way, sir.

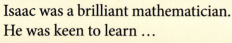

Isaac was a brilliant mathematician. He was keen to learn …

Almost 2000 years ago, the Ancient Greek philosopher Aristotle said every single thing is made of earth, air, fire and water.

Surely someone's come up with a new **theory** since then …?

Isaac soon grew weary of studying Ancient Greeks.

You ought to find out about René Descartes.

He's only been dead for twelve years – not 2000 like Aristotle.

Descartes worked out why rainbows appear. But not why they're different colours …

In 1665, the plague spread across England. The **authorities** started to limit travel.

Bring out yer dead!

Isaac headed for home in Lincolnshire.

Heading north, sir?

Yes. Be careful! There's valuable equipment inside.

Hello?

Welcome back, Master Isaac!

Safe from the plague, Isaac was free to let his mind wander.

I wonder …

… what makes the Moon …

… move through the sky like that?

Even though he was at home, Isaac continued to study hard.

More books for Master Isaac?

Yes – LOTS more.

He gathered information about comets …

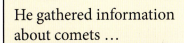

… the Moon …

… and the planets.

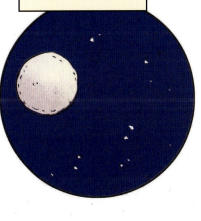

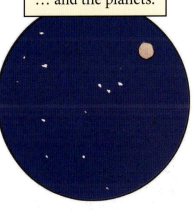

He worked out that one **force** affected all these bodies.

I shall call this 'Newton's Law of Universal Gravitation'.

In 1667, Isaac returned to Cambridge.

Trinity College that way …

I know!

His work on light and gravity soon made him the world's most famous scientist.

- Within two years of returning to Cambridge, Isaac had been made Professor of Mathematics at the university. He published *Principia Mathematica*, about the movement of planets and comets, and *Opticks*, about the behaviour of light. These two books changed science forever.

- Isaac also became the President of the Royal Society, a world-famous science institution based in London. Throughout his career Isaac fell out with several other scientists: he used his position as President to support his friends (which was good) and argue with his enemies (not so good).

- Isaac later became Master of the Mint, which put him in charge of the whole country's money. He oversaw 'recoinage', where all the old coins were taken in and replaced with new ones. Isaac's recoinage meant that English coins were in demand throughout Europe. This helped make the country's economy strong.

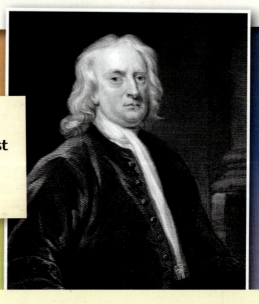

Isaac Newton
English mathematician and scientist
25th December 1642–
20th March 1727

Isaac's Law of Universal Gravitiation states that any two things in the universe 'attract' each other with a force of gravity.

Carl Linnaeus

I'm Carl Linnaeus. I developed a system for naming plants and animals. Yet I wasn't the best student at school …

Carl's father was summoned to his son's school in Sweden …

I wonder what he's done?

Carl keeps missing lessons.

He's never going to amount to anything.

Another teacher was more positive …

Carl is fascinated by living things. Could he become a doctor perhaps?

Hmm …

In 1728, Carl began studying to be a doctor at Uppsala University.

He was interested in the use of plants as medicines.

Such long names! It's fortunate I have a good memory.

Carl embarked on a journey north to discover Lapland's plants, animals and people.

He collected samples of previously unknown plants.

We need to keep moving …

Just a moment!

Campanula serpyllifolia
Linnea borealis?

Carl became friends with the Sami people.

They'll tell you about the local plants and animals.

Excellent!

The long summer up here in the Arctic is great – it's still light enough to sketch at midnight!

zzzzzz … zzzzzz … zzzzzz …

I've never seen one of THOSE before!

It's some sort of hawk owl! I'll call it *Surnia ulula*.

Of course, travelling through the north was sometimes gruelling … particularly in winter.

Brrrr!

Watch out!

KER-RUNCH!

Err – we might need to go another way?

Hmm …

There's no food left.

Despite the hardships, by the time he got home, Carl had discovered hundreds of new plants and animals.

I just need to compile my notes. Then they can be published.

Carl Linnaeus
Swedish biologist and doctor
23rd May 1707–
10th January 1778

- The new plants and animals that Carl discovered in Lapland all needed names: this gave Carl a chance to put into practice his ideas about a new way of naming living things.

- In Carl's new system, each living thing had two Latin names. The first name says which group of animals or plants the thing belongs to. The second name identifies which member of the group it is. For example, the owl on page 10 is *Surnia* (hawk owl) *ulula* (from the north) – a northern hawk owl. Carl's naming system worked so well that it was taken up by scientists everywhere, and is still used today.

- Carl became a professor at Uppsala University. He continued to explore Lapland and to write science books: in his lifetime he wrote a total of 72.

- Carl was knighted for his services to Sweden: he was no longer plain old Carl Linnaeus, but instead was known as Carl von Linné.

Michael Faraday

I'm Michael Faraday. From a young age I loved science and was particularly fascinated by electricity!

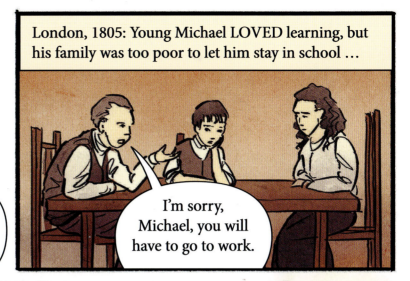

London, 1805: Young Michael LOVED learning, but his family was too poor to let him stay in school …

I'm sorry, Michael, you will have to go to work.

Michael went to work for a bookseller. He spent all day delivering books …

These are for Mr Farquharson.

I'll see he gets them.

… and most of the night reading them.

This is even better than school!

A few years later …

If you have such an appetite for science, you should go to this talk.

At the ROYAL INSTITUTION SIR HUMPHRY DAVY will lecture upon the FOREMOST SCIENTIFIC PROBLEMS of the day including EXPERIMENTS in CHEMISTRY.

Sir Humphry Davy's lectures were very exciting.

Michael was hooked! He attended every lecture he could.

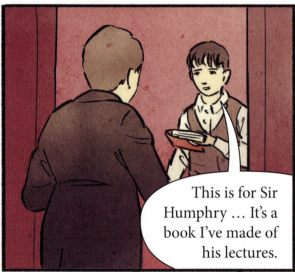

This is for Sir Humphry … It's a book I've made of his lectures.

In Sir Humphry's laboratory …

Ow! My hand!

BANG!

I won't be able to write with this. I need a **scribe**. Maybe the boy who made the book would like a job?

First, Michael became Sir Humphry's scribe.

So, the problem of acidity …

Then he became his chemical assistant.

Soon, Michael was working on his own scientific ideas.

FLASH!

BANG!

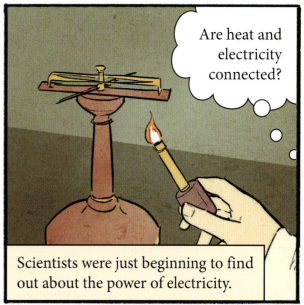

Are heat and electricity connected?

Scientists were just beginning to find out about the power of electricity.

Michael began to ponder how to MAKE electricity.

A copper wheel … wires … a big magnet … What happens when the wheel spins?

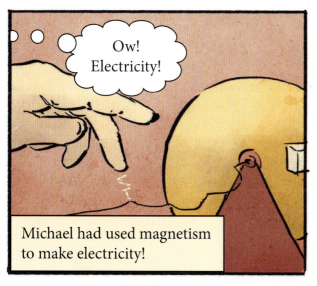

Ow! Electricity!

Michael had used magnetism to make electricity!

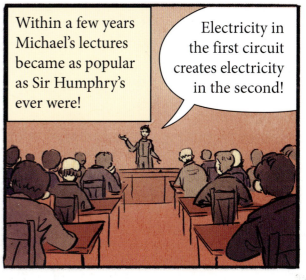

Within a few years Michael's lectures became as popular as Sir Humphry's ever were!

Electricity in the first circuit creates electricity in the second!

- Michael was one of the most famous scientists of his day. He became Director of the Royal Institution's Laboratory, and Professor of Chemistry. He was responsible for many scientific developments we still use today.

- Every time you use electricity, it's a reminder of Michael who developed the first electrical motors and discovered the science of electrical generators. Also, whenever you open a fridge and take out a cold drink, think of Michael: he first used mechanical pumps to turn gas into liquid, then back to gas. This process lowers the temperature, and is how modern fridges work.

- Michael was also interested in the environment. He investigated the effects of industrial pollution in Wales, and wrote to the newspapers about the terrible pollution of the River Thames.

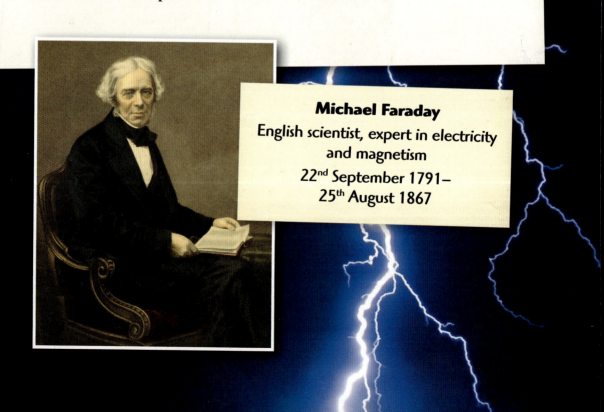

Michael Faraday
English scientist, expert in electricity and magnetism
22nd September 1791–
25th August 1867

Marie Curie

I'm Marie Curie. I became the first woman ever to win a Nobel Prize in Science. Then I won another!

In 1867, Poland was controlled by Russia.

WAAA!

In the capital, Warsaw, two teachers had a baby daughter. They called her Marie.

As Marie grew up she started helping with science experiments in the kitchen.

So, when we heat the mixture …

It changes colour!

Marie LOVED studying …

This year's most outstanding student is … Marie! Well done!

Marie dreamed of going to university, but there was an obstacle in her way …

Warsaw University

No women allowed

For Marie to get to university, she needed a plan …

While she saved, Marie studied at Warsaw's secret 'Floating University'.

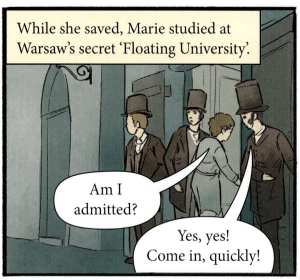

The classes were in subjects banned under Russian rule. The locations of the classes were always changing, so that the authorities wouldn't find them.

Finally, Marie saved enough money to go to Paris.

She arrived at Gare de l'Est station on her way to the Sorbonne.

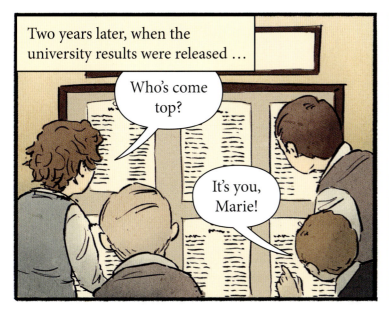

Two years later, when the university results were released …

Who's come top?

It's you, Marie!

Marie started to investigate electricity and magnets.

How did THAT happen?

She met another magnet expert, Pierre. They fell in love and were married.

They also started working together.

I can't see the rays …

… but I know they're there!

Marie became fascinated with pitchblende – a rock that releases invisible rays.

Marie found that *something* in pitchblende gave off an electric charge: she wanted to know what.

Marie and Pierre broke up hundreds of tons of rock.

Finally, they found the source of the rays …

Marie named the discovery after her homeland, Poland.

A few months later she discovered another element …

The radioactive rays could be used to take 'X-ray' pictures of a person's INSIDES!

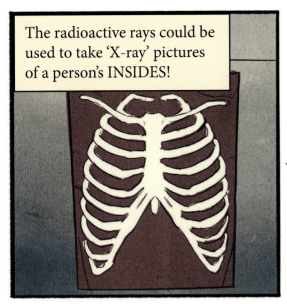

In 1914, World War One began ...

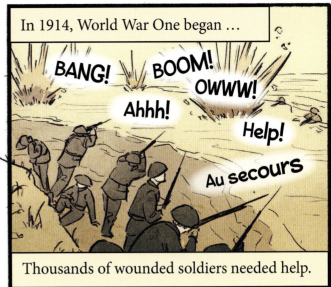

Thousands of wounded soldiers needed help.

The X-ray trucks were known as *Petites Curies* – 'little Curies'. Marie and her daughter, Irene, set up the trucks close to the battlefield.

If we had trucks with equipment for taking X-rays they could go wherever they were needed.

Ready?

Yes, ready.

A million soldiers visited the Petites Curies. The X-ray trucks saved thousands of lives.

Marie Curie
Polish physicist and chemist
7th November 1867–
4th July 1934

- Marie and Pierre's work on radiation led to them winning the Nobel Prize for Physics in 1903. They shared it with Henri Becquerel, who had first discovered the rays existed, but not what they were. At first the judges wanted to give the prize only to Pierre and Becquerel – but Pierre insisted Marie had to share in it.

- When Pierre died in 1906, Marie took over his job of Professor of Physics at the Sorbonne University. She continued her work, and in 1911 was given a *second* Nobel Prize. This time it was for chemistry, in recognition of her work on the elements radium and polonium.

- Today, radiation treatment is used to stop many forms of deadly cancers. The rays kill cancerous cells, and prevent the disease spreading through a person's body. Marie's discoveries and work have now saved the lives of millions of people.

Albert Einstein

I'm Albert Einstein. I came up with complicated theories that changed the way scientists thought about subjects such as light, gravity and time.

Germany, 1893 …

Sunbeams! Light travels so fast that we can't see it move …

Einstein! Are you paying attention?

Albert would spend a lot of time daydreaming …

If you ran at the speed of light, what would light look like? A straight line?

Or waves?

However, his daydreams didn't help him pass his exams …

At university, Albert missed lots of lectures as he was busy with his own studies!

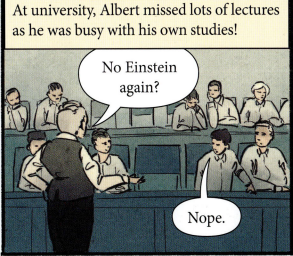

No Einstein again?

Nope.

1902, in Zurich, Switzerland …

Albert was working at the **patent office**.

One day, Albert was pondering a complex theory with his friend, Michele Besso.

I've been thinking about an old idea – but I'm a bit stuck.

Yes?

It was to do with time and motion.

One thing's for sure …

It's not a problem you can solve overnight!

I wonder if …

It wasn't easy, but Albert persevered with the problem.

The next day …

Good morning! I have completely solved the problem.

What?!

I think I'll call my theory … Special Relativity!

Albert published it in 1905.

Special Relativity was a huge shake-up in the science world.

No! No! No!

Impossible!

Just look at the equations!

It changed the way scientists thought about time and motion forever.

Eleven years later, Albert added to his original ideas …

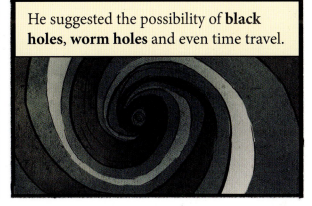

He suggested the possibility of **black holes**, **worm holes** and even time travel.

Over fifty years later, the first black hole was discovered.

The data shows us that Einstein was right!

Albert also came up with the world's most famous equation …

Got it! $E = mc^2$

It's a complicated equation that links mass and energy.

It helped to explain where the Sun and other stars got their energy from.

It also helped to develop **nuclear energy**.

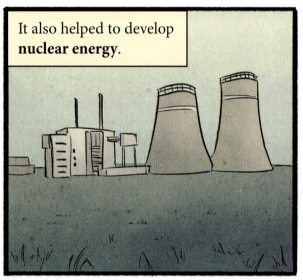

Some scientists also used Albert's equation to create an **atomic bomb**, which he was upset by.

Science should be used for good!

Albert became the most famous scientist in the world.

Eventually, the fame became too much for Albert. When stopped in the street he would say …

Always I am being confused with this Albert Einstein!

… then he would hurry off!

- Albert's paper on Special Relativity was just one of *four* game-changing science papers he wrote in only one year (1905). He went from being an unknown clerk in a patent office to being talked about by every scientist on the planet.

- Albert received the Nobel Prize in Physics in 1921, although it wasn't for his most famous and influential discovery of Relativity. He actually won the Nobel Prize for his discovery of the law of the photoelectric effect.

- Einstein's theories lie behind many of the inventions we use today. Without them, we wouldn't have GPS systems, accurate clocks or automatic doors, for example.

- Albert loved to play the violin. He often said that if he had not been a physicist, he would have been a musician.

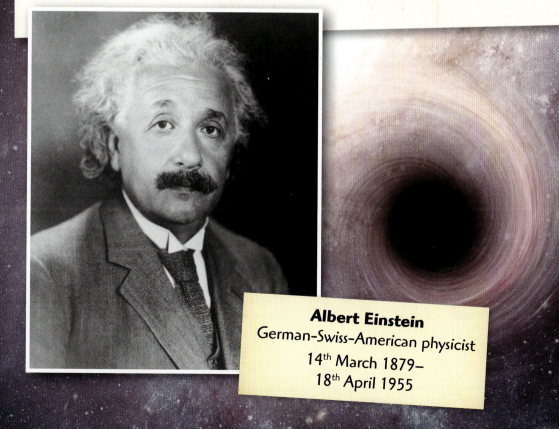

Albert Einstein
German–Swiss–American physicist
14th March 1879–
18th April 1955

Alexander Fleming

I'm Dr Alexander Fleming, and I made one of the greatest accidental scientific discoveries ever!

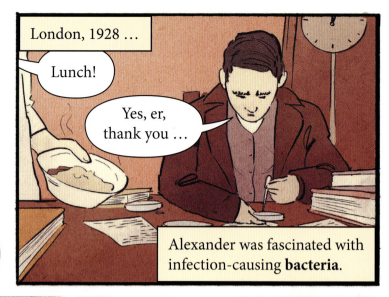

London, 1928 …

Lunch!

Yes, er, thank you …

Alexander was fascinated with infection-causing **bacteria**.

It's easy to get distracted, when there are millions of bacteria to study …

I'm hungry. Time for lunch!

Oh dear, it's gone cold. Again.

Alexander, I've come to take you home. You're working late again.

You need a break from bacteria! It's time for a holiday.

Maybe you're right.

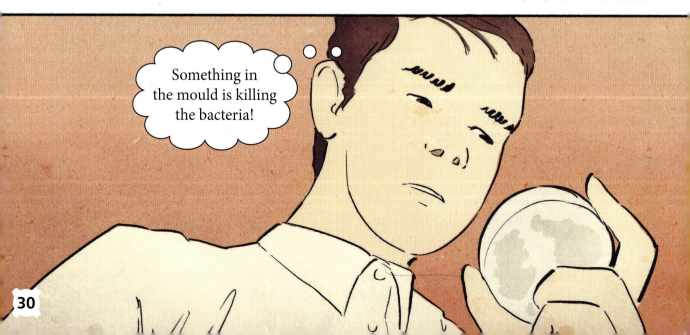

I'll call my new bacteria-killer 'mould juice'. Just think of all the things it could help cure!

In the end, he decided 'penicillin' was less likely to put people off!

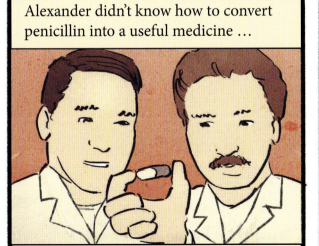

Alexander didn't know how to convert penicillin into a useful medicine …

… but fortunately some other scientists, Howard Florey and Ernst Chain, did.

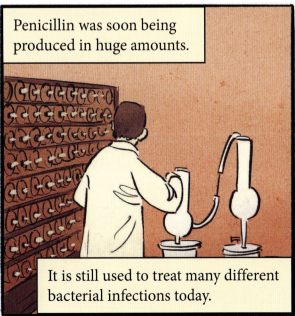

Penicillin was soon being produced in huge amounts.

It is still used to treat many different bacterial infections today.

Alexander Fleming
Scottish scientist
6th August 1881–
11th March 1955

- Penicillin wasn't the only discovery Alexander made accidentally. In 1921 he found a new **antiseptic** chemical in nasal mucus.

- Penicillin was the first antibiotic medicine. Antibiotics help the human body fight off bacterial infections and diseases. These include everything from toothache and pneumonia to boils or broken limbs. Penicillin is still commonly used today.

- In October 1945 – seventeen years after Alexander discovered penicillin – he, Howard Florey and Ernst Chain were awarded the Nobel Prize in recognition of their work on developing the drug that by then had saved millions of lives.

Alan Turing

I'm Alan Turing. My code-breaking work is believed to have shortened World War Two by two whole years!

World War Two: Buckinghamshire, England.

We *will* need to see your face, sir …

Yes, OK.

Morning, Gordon.

Morning Prof.

Bletchley Park was an important strategic site where a crucial battle was being fought …

… the battle to crack Germany's secret Enigma codes.

Britain's most formidable weapon had arrived at work …

Hay fever bad this morning, Prof?

Terrible!

… a code-breaker called Alan Turing – also known as 'Prof'.

As the code-breakers worked, the Battle of the Atlantic raged.

German U-boat 'wolf packs' were sinking hundreds of supply ships.

Torpedos auswärts!

Torpedoes away!

The U-boats communicated using a code called Enigma.

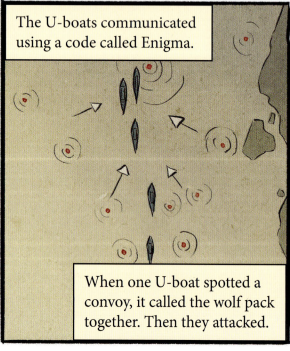

When one U-boat spotted a convoy, it called the wolf pack together. Then they attacked.

U-Boats Sink More Ships

If we could just crack Enigma, we'd know where they are!

In the North Atlantic: 9th May 1941 …

A German U-boat was captured by the British Navy.

An Engima machine and its code books were seized.

Even after breaking the code, working out what the messages said was very laborious.

Alan had designed 'Bombe' machines to help decode Enigma …

… but there weren't enough operators.

The Prime Minister, Winston Churchill, received a letter from Alan requesting help.

Elizabeth! Come and take a memo!

Winston wrote to the Head of the Army …

PRIME MINISTER'S OFFICE

From: Prime Minister
To: General Hastings Ismay, Army Chief of Staff
Subject: Bletchley Park
ACTION THIS DAY!

Make sure they have all they want on extreme priority and report to me that this has been done.

The letter worked! Soon the Bombes had plenty of operators.

More from the Bombes.

Thanks.

We seem to be winning at last, Prof.

More **decrypts** every day.

More decrypts – and fewer supply ships sunk.

The work of Turing and his colleagues saved millions of lives.

- Today Alan is famous for his work on breaking German codes during World War Two. This work may even have changed history: if the Battle of the Atlantic had been lost, Britain might have surrendered. That was why Britain's wartime Prime Minister, Winston Churchill, once said that: "The only thing that really frightened me during the war was the U-boat peril."

- Alan is also famous as one of the first computer scientists. In 1936, he had invented what became known as the 'Turing machine' – a machine that could decode instructions and carry them out. Then, in 1946, Alan designed the 'Automatic Computing Engine', a digital computer.

- In 1950, Alan developed what is now called the 'Turing test' for artificial intelligence (whether a machine can think). The test was based on whether or not a computer could fool a human questioner into thinking the machine was human.

Alan Turing
English mathematician and computer expert
23rd June 1912–
7th June 1954

Back at the museum

I am Christiaan Huygens. My main scientific discovery was that light travels in waves. But I was also fascinated by time and clocks.

My name is Robert Hooke. I designed a microscope that let me see tiny parts of the natural world.

I am Gottfried Wilhelm Leibniz, and I developed the binary number system, which is still used today in digital code. I also invented a mechanical arithmetic machine.

My name is Alessandro Volta. I am famous for inventing the electric battery.

I'm Ada Lovelace, often known as 'the first computer programmer' – even though I lived 100 years before computers were invented!

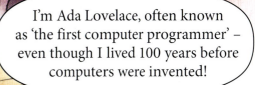

I'm James Clerk Maxwell. My work on light, electricity and magnetism, and temperature was groundbreaking. I also produced the first ever colour photograph!

My name is Rachel Carson. As a marine biologist and environmental campaigner, I let the world know the harm some farming chemicals were doing to the natural world.

I am Stephen Hawking. My best-known work is on black holes and the origins of the universe. I wrote a bestselling book called *A Brief History of Time*.

Glossary

antiseptic   preventing micro-organisms that cause diseases from growing

atomic bomb   a nuclear weapon that releases a huge amount of energy by splitting atoms in certain elements

authority   a person or organization in power

bacteria   micro-organisms, some kinds of which can make you ill

black hole   an area of space with such strong gravity that no light can escape

corrupt   to change or alter something, usually for the worse

decrypt   a decoded message

element   a basic building block of any material

force   an influence on something that affects how it moves

luminous   giving off light; bright or shining

nuclear energy   energy created by splitting atoms in certain elements

patent office   a place where copyrights are granted

pneumonia   inflamed lung caused by infection

radioactivity   what occurs when substances give off certain dangerous particles

scribe   a person who copies out documents or writes things down

theory   an idea or group of ideas that explains something

worm hole   an imagined 'hole' or connection between different places in time and space

Index